Weiss Ratings' Consumer Guide to Term Life Insurance

Weiss Ratings' Consumer Guide to Term Life Insurance

Fall 2022

GREY HOUSE PUBLISHING

Weiss Ratings
4400 Northcorp Parkway
Palm Beach Gardens, FL 33410
561-627-3300

Published by Grey House Publishing, Inc., located at 4919 Route 22, Amenia, NY 12501; telephone 518-789-8700. Grey House Publishing neither guarantees the accuracy of the data contained herein nor assumes any responsibility for errors, omissions or discrepancies. Grey House Publishing accepts no payment for listing; inclusion in the publication of any organization, agency, institution, publication, service or individual does not imply endorsement of the publisher.

4919 Route 22
PO Box 56
Amenia, NY 12501-0056

Fall 2022 Edition

ISBN: 978-1-63700-201-8
ISSN: 2164-3105

CONTENTS

Terms and Conditions

This document is prepared strictly for the confidential use of our customer(s). It has been provided to you at your specific request. It is not directed to, or intended for distribution to or use by, any person or entity who is a citizen or resident of or located in any locality, state, country or other jurisdiction where such distribution, publication, availability or use would be contrary to law or regulation or which would subject Weiss Ratings, LLC or its affiliates to any registration or licensing requirement within such jurisdiction.

No part of the analysts' compensation was, is, or will be, directly or indirectly, related to the specific recommendations or views expressed in this research report.

This document is not intended for the direct or indirect solicitation of business. Weiss Ratings, LLC, and its affiliates disclaim any and all liability to any person or entity for any loss or damage caused, in whole or in part, by any error (negligent or otherwise) or other circumstances involved in, resulting from or relating to the procurement, compilation, analysis, interpretation, editing, transcribing, publishing and/or dissemination or transmittal of any information contained herein.

Weiss Ratings, LLC has not taken any steps to ensure that the securities or investment vehicle referred to in this report are suitable for any particular investor. The investment or services contained or referred to in this report may not be suitable for you and it is recommended that you consult an independent investment advisor if you are in doubt about such investments or investment services. Nothing in this report constitutes investment, legal, accounting or tax advice or a representation that any investment or strategy is suitable or appropriate to your individual circumstances or otherwise constitutes a personal recommendation to you.

The ratings and other opinions contained in this document must be construed solely as statements of opinion from Weiss Ratings, LLC, and not statements of fact. Each rating or opinion must be weighed solely as a factor in your choice of an institution and should not be construed as a recommendation to buy, sell or otherwise act with respect to the particular product or company involved.

Past performance should not be taken as an indication or guarantee of future performance, and no representation or warranty, expressed or implied, is made regarding future performance. Information, opinions and estimates contained in this report reflect a judgment at its original date of publication and are subject to change without notice. Weiss Ratings, LLC offers a notification service for rating changes on companies you specify. For more information visit WeissRatings.com or call 1-877-934-7778. The price, value and income from any of the securities or financial instruments mentioned in this report can fall as well as rise.

This document and the information contained herein is copyrighted by Weiss Ratings, LLC. Any copying, displaying, selling, distributing or otherwise delivering of this information or any part of this document to any other person or entity is prohibited without the express written consent of Weiss Ratings, LLC, with the exception of a reviewer or editor who may quote brief passages in connection with a review or a news story.

Part I:

Do You Need
Life Insurance?

Introduction

As you probably well know, purchasing life insurance is one of the easiest activities to procrastinate. In fact, most people must go through some life-altering event before they're even willing to talk about life insurance, much less act on it. For instance, you may have recently gotten married, had children, or had a health scare, making you think about how your loved ones would fare in the event of your untimely passing. Whatever the reason, it is in your own best interest to educate yourself about life insurance beforehand so you can buy exactly what you need and can afford, rather than what some salesman is selling.

About this Guide

That's where Weiss Ratings can help. This *Consumer Guide to Term Life Insurance* is designed to give you a good overview of your life insurance options, particularly in the area of term life. It walks you through the considerations for selecting the appropriate type, amount, and term of the insurance. And then it walks you through the purchasing process of buying a life insurance policy. And, lastly we provide a list of Weiss Recommended Life and Health Insurers.

Best of all, you can rest assured that the information presented here is completely independent and free of bias. Weiss Ratings does not sell insurance, we are not connected with any insurance companies, and we won't make a single penny should you decide to purchase a policy from one of the companies in this guide. As a matter of fact, we don't care if you decide to purchase an insurance policy or not. Our goal is to simply help you make the best decision possible – for you and your family's needs.

When Does Life Insurance Make Sense?

Contrary to what many insurers will tell you, not everyone truly needs life insurance. In its purest form, life insurance is merely a form of financial protection in the event of your death. You sign a contract to pay premiums to an insurance company and in return, the company agrees to provide a specified amount of money (i.e. benefit) to whomever you designate (i.e. your beneficiary(ies), upon your passing.

This financial protection can be particularly comforting when it comes to providing …

- protection for your family against financial hardship or to maintain their current standard of living.

- cash to pay off mortgages, taxes, or other debts so your heirs are not left with them.

- funds to pay funeral expenses.

- a continuing income stream for your surviving family members.

- an inheritance for your heirs.

- a nest egg for future expenses like your children's or grandchildren's education.

As you can see, life insurance is most applicable when you have dependents or heirs that you want to provide for. On the other hand, there are plenty of situations when life insurance does not make sense. For instance…

- **If you are single and don't have any dependents**, you probably don't need life insurance. A salesman may try to persuade you to purchase a policy with arguments like:

  - the premiums are lower while you are young, so it makes sense to lock them in now,

    or

  - by purchasing a long-term policy now, you will not have to provide evidence of insurability later.

While both of these statements are true, odds are you'll be paying premiums needlessly if you follow this line of reasoning. If you truly don't need life insurance now, then why pay for it? And what are the chances that your health will take a significant turn for the worse before you reach the point when you do need life insurance? It's your money, but if you want to hang onto as much of it as possible, don't buy insurance before you can demonstrate a real need for it.

- **If you are retired and have no dependents**, you probably don't need life insurance. At this time in your life, you most likely don't have large debts (like a big mortgage) or dependents relying on your income. If there is no one who will be financially harmed when you pass away, then why spend money on life insurance when you could be spending it on yourself or some other worthwhile cause. Plus, premiums for people over age 65 are very high and may even be unaffordable. An exception to this logic may apply if you are using life insurance as an estate planning tool to avoid taxes.

- **If your spouse has a high enough income** and could maintain his or her standard of living without your contribution, then you probably don't need life insurance. Life insurance should be purchased to replace the income or services you're currently providing for your family. However, if your family would not be financially harmed by your death, then it doesn't make sense to spend money on life insurance (unless done for estate planning reasons).

- **If you are considering a policy for a minor child**, then he or she probably does not need life insurance unless you would need the money to cover basic funeral expenses. Undoubtedly the loss of a child would be terribly tragic. Financially speaking though, you would not experience a loss of income provided by the child. Therefore, life insurance does not make sense for minor children except as insurance against the cost of funeral expenses.

At the other end of the spectrum, if you have young children, a spouse, or other family members who are relying on your contribution to the household income in order to pay the bills, then you probably do need life insurance. At this point, the question becomes…

Part II:

What Type of Life Insurance Policy Makes the Most Sense for You?

Finding the Type of Policy You Need

Life insurance comes in many flavors, each designed to suit a specific need. For instance, there are policies that will pay off the balance on your mortgage. There are policies that will provide your family with a specified income stream for a fixed number of years after your death. There are policies where the benefit goes up in value as you get older. And there are even policies where the benefit goes down in value as you get older.

When you boil it all down though, there are really only two fundamental types of life insurance policies: permanent life and term life.

Permanent Life

As the name would suggest, permanent life is a *lifetime* insurance policy. You might also think of it as life insurance with a savings account built in. With permanent life, a portion of the premiums you pay to the insurance company go toward establishing a "cash value" which can be withdrawn if you cancel the policy or may potentially be used to pay for future premiums on the policy. And unless you exhaust your cash value, your beneficiaries are guaranteed to receive the death benefit when you pass.

So in a way, a permanent life policy is like an investment with a life insurance component. It is particularly useful for individuals who are concerned about their ability to pay premiums in later years or for those lacking the discipline to establish a separate savings plan.

Term Life

Term life, on the other hand, provides insurance coverage for only a specified period of time. The death benefit is only paid if you die during that specified term and have paid the required premiums. At the end of the term, however, the policy expires and you walk away with nothing to show. There is no cash value built up and your insurance coverage ceases to exist unless you purchase another policy.

In other words, term life insurance provides temporary coverage. If you live past the end of the term, you will have made years of premium payments but receive no money in return from the insurer. Of course, if you were to die at the beginning of the term, you would have paid very little in the way of premiums and yet the insurance company would have to pay your beneficiaries the full policy benefit.

At first blush, term life insurance may not sound as appealing as permanent life. That is, until you get to the cost. The premiums for a term life policy can be considerably less expensive than those for a permanent life policy. That's because with term life, you're not contributing anything extra to build up a cash value. Instead, you're only paying for the insurance coverage plus the insurer's administrative expenses.

Thus term life makes the most sense for people who only need life insurance for a limited amount of time, such as until the children are grown and earning their own living, until the mortgage is paid off, or until the family can afford to carry on without your financial contribution.

If you're still intrigued by the permanent, lifetime nature of permanent life, many financial advisors suggest that disciplined savers are better off purchasing a term policy and investing the extra premium dollars that you would have spent on a permanent policy. This methodology is essentially the same thing as permanent life – i.e. insurance with a savings component – except that the savings component is not directly tied to the policy, giving you much more freedom in how you invest and use the funds. Assuming you make prudent investment choices, you could then use the amount invested, plus any added investment earnings, to pay future premiums on a term policy.

Term Life Policy Features

Once you make the decision that term life is right for you, then you must consider any added policy features that you're willing to pay for. Options available typically include:

- **Renewable Term**

  A renewable term life policy will allow you to add another term onto the policy when the current term expires, thus extending the term of coverage. This renewal provision usually requires that you extend the policy for the same term and the same face amount as the original policy because you are older, but you usually won't be required to submit any new evidence of insurability (i.e. no medical exams or health history questionnaires).

- **Convertible Term**

  A convertible term life policy will allow you to convert the policy from a term policy to a permanent policy at some point in the future without requiring new evidence of insurability. This feature can be appealing if you would really prefer a permanent life policy, with its savings component, but can't currently afford the higher premiums.

- **Waiver of Premium Rider**

  A rider is an addendum to the policy that can either expand or limit the policy's benefits, with a corresponding increase or decrease in premium. A waiver of premium rider will allow you to skip your premium payments if you become disabled, thus enabling you to keep the policy in force even when you can't work and make money to pay the premiums.

- **Spouse Rider**

  A spouse rider will provide insurance coverage for your spouse in addition to yourself. This may be appealing if you need coverage for both yourself and your spouse since it will typically cost less than purchasing two separate policies.

- **Children's Rider**

  Similar to the spouse rider, a children's rider will provide insurance coverage for your children in addition to yourself. In addition to the added coverage being cheaper, this rider typically covers all of your children, no matter how many you have, for one premium amount. Additionally, many children's riders will allow the child to convert the policy to his or her own life insurance policy at a specified age, without requiring evidence of insurability.

Life Insurance Policy Types

As discussed previously, life insurance policies generally fall into one of two broad categories: permanent life or term life. Within these categories, however, there are a multitude of options that allow you to customize the policy to meet your specific needs – at either higher or reduced premium costs depending on the type of policy. This report does not (and could not possibly) provide premium rates for each of these policy variations, so if you see a policy type that appeals to you, be sure to inquire if it is available when you begin working with an insurer or agent.

Term Life Policy Types

- **Level Term Insurance** provides life insurance coverage for a specified number of years, typically a 5, 10, 15, or 20-year term. Both the death benefit and the annual premium remain the same over the course of the term you can cancel the policy at any time during the term. Parts 2 through 5 of this report provide premium rates for level term policies available to you.

Level Term

	Annual Premium	Death Benefit
Year 1	$400	$300,000
Year 2	$400	$300,000
Year 3	$400	$300,000
Year 4	$400	$300,000
Year 5	$400	$300,000

The benefit of a level term policy is that you can lock in your premium without having to worry about a yearly rate increase. That means you will typically pay more in the early years for a level term policy compared to a yearly renewable term policy, but pay less in the later years of the term.

- **<u>Yearly Renewable Term (YRT) Insurance</u>**, also called Annually Renewable Term (ART), provides life insurance coverage for only one year. At the end of that year, the policy expires but may be renewed for an additional year at a slightly higher premium rate. This allows you to pay as little as possible in the early years of coverage while paying more in the later years.

Yearly Renewable Term

	Annual Premium	Death Benefit
Year 1	$380	$300,000
Year 2	$395	$300,000
Year 3	$410	$300,000
Year 4	$425	$300,000
Year 5	$475	$300,000

This type of policy is most appealing to individuals who can't afford the higher premiums of a level term policy, only require coverage for a few years, or want to remain flexible with their coverage term.

- **<u>Decreasing Term Insurance</u>**, also called Annually Renewable Term (ART), is just the opposite of yearly renewable term. Here the annual premiums remain the same throughout the term of the policy, but the death benefit declines annually due to the higher mortality rate as you get older.

Decreasing Term

	Annual Premium	Death Benefit
Year 1	$400	$400,000
Year 2	$400	$305,000
Year 3	$400	$300,000
Year 4	$400	$280,000
Year 5	$400	$240,000

This type of policy is most appealing to individuals who expect their savings and investments to grow each year, effectively lessening the amount of life insurance coverage they need.

Two common types of decreasing term policies are **Mortgage Redemption** and **Credit Life** insurance. With mortgage redemption insurance, the death benefit equals and declines in tandem with the decreasing balance of your mortgage loan. Credit life is similar although it is typically tied to other types of loans like automobile or credit card loans.

- **Increasing Term Insurance**, provides a death benefit that periodically increases throughout the term of the policy. For example, many increasing term policies are indexed to increase the death benefit annually at the same rate as the Consumer Price Index (CPI) in order to keep pace with inflation. This gives you the comfort of knowing that the policy benefit will always be sufficient to cover your dependents' needs, regardless of inflation.

Increasing Term

	Annual Premium	Death Benefit
Year 1	$380	$300,000
Year 2	$400	$305,000
Year 3	$420	$310,000
Year 4	$475	$315,000
Year 5	$305	$300,000

To compensate for this added protection, however, the policy premiums will also increase each year.

- **Family Income Insurance** provides your beneficiaries with a death benefit that comes in the form of a monthly payment until the end of the term rather than the typical lump sum. This can be particularly attractive if you are concerned about your spouse's ability to manage a lump sum payment and make it last for an extended number of years.

There are several other types of term life policies which are slight variations on the policies previously described. Usually, they are niche policies that have been designed to meet a very specific post-death need. Regardless, they all have two things in common:

1) Term life policies always have an expiration, after which you must renew the policy, purchase a new one, or drop the coverage; and

2) With term life you are paying only for the insurance coverage and the insurer's administrative expenses. That means you are not contributing toward a savings plan or other form of investment.

Permanent Life Policy Types

- **Whole Life Insurance** provides lifetime coverage with a fixed death benefit and a fixed, level premium. As the years pass, a portion of your premium contributions are set aside as savings, and your accumulated savings can then be borrowed against, withdrawn by canceling the

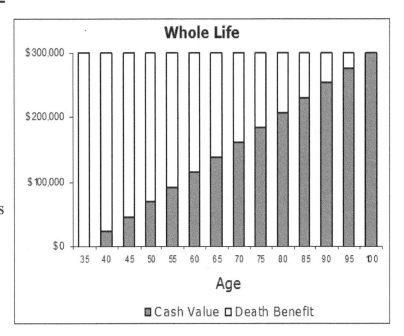

policy, or applied by the insurance company toward paying the policy benefit upon death. Eventually, the cash value will build up to equal the death benefit at which time it is returned to the policyholder, usually at age 100.

For example, the Whole Life graph illustrates the growing cash value for a hypothetical $300,000 whole life policy purchased at age 35. If the insured were to die at age 40, the death benefit received by his beneficiaries would be $300,000 of which roughly $25,000 would come from the policy's accumulated cash value and the remaining $275,000 would come from the policy's insurance coverage.

- **Modified Whole Life Insurance** is similar to whole life insurance except that you are able to set it up with a changing premium payment and/or death benefit. This is particularly attractive if you want a whole

Modified Whole Life

	Annual Premium	Death Benefit
Years 1 – 20	$2,000	$300,000
Years 21+	$6,000	$300,000

life policy but can't currently afford the premium for the death benefit your family needs. For example, a hypothetical $300,000 policy that would normally require a $3,000

annual premium may be modified so that you pay only $2,000 in premiums per year for the first 20 years and then $6,000 per year for the remainder of the policy.

- **Joint Whole Life Insurance**, also known as "first-to-die" life insurance, works the same way as whole life insurance except that it provides coverage for two people. At the death of either insured, the death benefit is paid to the surviving insured and the policy terminates.

- **Last Survivor Whole Life Insurance**, also known as "second-to-die" life insurance, is similar to joint life except that it pays the death benefit only after both insured's have died. This type of policy is useful for married couples who want to provide their heirs with the funds necessary to pay estate taxes.

- **Universal Life Insurance** is similar to whole life insurance except that it allows you to vary the amount of your annual premium contribution or suspend it altogether, if you choose. As a result, the cash value and the death benefit will fluctuate, depending on the adequacy of your premium payments. There are three main components to a universal life policy:

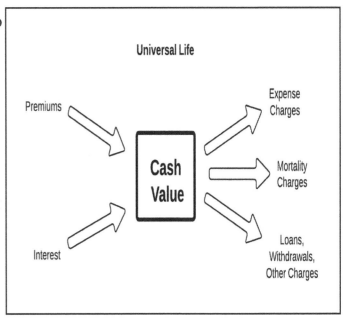

(1) mortality charges, (2) interest credited to the cash value, and (3) expense charges. The mortality charges pay for the insurance coverage. The interest is earned by your cash value in the policy, similar to a savings account. The expense charges cover the insurance company's administrative expenses. Any loans, withdrawals, or other expenses are also subtracted from the cash value. The diagram above shows how all these factors relate to one another. The premiums you pay and the interest earned on your cash value flow into the cash value. The mortality charges, administrative expense charges, loans, withdrawals, and other expenses flow out of the cash value. People with fluctuating incomes, such as commissioned sales people, usually find this type of policy attractive.

- **<u>Variable Life Insurance</u>** is a combination of (a) regular whole life insurance, and (b) an investment account. That's because you control how the cash value of your policy is invested, not the insurance company. Using your accumulated cash value, you can invest in stock, bond, and money market mutual funds, on a tax-deferred basis. This type of policy generally appeals more to risk takers who are willing to assume a degree of market risk in order to hopefully pay less in premiums.

- **<u>Variable Universal Life Insurance</u>** is basically the same as variable life insurance with one key difference: a variable universal life policy allows you to vary the amount of your annual premium or suspend it altogether, if you choose.

  As a result, the cash value and amount of insurance coverage fluctuate, depending on the adequacy of your premium payments.

There are of course other types of permanent life insurance policies designed to accommodate specific needs. You will find, however, that they are simply variations on the policies previously described. Be aware though that the more gimmicks you get incorporated into a policy, the more you will pay for your insurance coverage relative to these more simple policy types.

How Much Life Insurance and for How Long?

In most instances, a term life policy will meet your specific needs at the lowest overall dollar cost. So the next step is to determine exactly how much insurance you need and for how long. These are the two primary factors that you control when determining what you will be required to pay in premiums. One other factor, your health, will also influence your premium rate, but that's not something you're going to be able to select.

<u>Death Benefit</u>

Assuming you can afford it, you should be looking to purchase a policy with a death benefit that when combined with your savings would enable your dependents to theoretically pay off all current debts (funeral expenses, taxes, loans, etc.) and future expenses (ongoing income needs, children's education, etc.). Current or expected debts are relatively easy to figure. It's those future expenses that

are a little more difficult to get a handle on.

Things to consider include:

- the age of your children,

- your current standard of living,

- what might be an acceptable standard of living for your surviving dependents, and

- expected inflation.

If you have young children, you will probably need more life insurance than someone whose children are in college. And if you expect to trade up to a bigger house with a bigger mortgage, you'll also need more life insurance than someone who has no such aspirations. Conversely, if your spouse comes from humble beginnings and would feel comfortable returning to a lower standard of living, then you can probably get by with less life insurance.

In the end, determining the amount of insurance you need is not an exact science. We have included a worksheet in the Appendix that will help you get to a good ballpark figure. If you've got a sizable estate though, or if you are uncomfortable following our worksheet, you should seek the advice of a qualified fee-only estate planner (see www.NAPFA.org for a list of estate planners near you).

Policy Term

Once you get a handle on the size of the policy needed, the next step is to determine how long it will take until your family could get by with a significantly lower benefit, or none at all. This will vary greatly depending on your individual circumstances, such as the age of your children or the number of years before you retire.

For example, most experts will advise you to choose a term that will at least last until your youngest child turns 18 or when that child might be expected to graduate from college. You may ultimately decide upon a longer term, but this recommended minimum term will at least provide coverage until a point in time when your family's needs are likely to change. At that time, you may be able to move to a policy with a lower death benefit.

Likewise, many people base their policy term on their number of years until retirement. The reasoning here is that upon retirement, your dependents will be able to tap into your accumulated retirement funds as a source of income, making the insurance unnecessary.

As with the death benefit, selecting an appropriate term is not an exact science. You should select whatever you feel will adequately provide for your dependents without extending too far beyond any expected needs changing events. You can always choose to cancel, or non-renew, the policy if you no longer need it. But be aware that the longer the term you select up front, the more expensive the policy will be.

Part III:

Things to Consider When Looking for the Right Policy

Once you have a handle on the amount of insurance and the term you need, you're ready to go shopping. Here are the things you need to consider as you look for a policy:

Your Health

If you are in relatively good health, you should have no problem finding a good policy at a good price. All insurance companies will require you to fill out paperwork detailing your medical history, and many will even require a physical exam, particularly if you are considering a large death benefit. Unfortunately there is no way to get around this screening process, so plan to spend some time consulting your medical records. And be sure to save a copy of your finished paperwork in order to make it easier the next time around if you should decide to apply for a different policy.

Be advised that some insurers are more selective than others, so just because one company classifies you as "standard" health, don't assume that classification will carry over to a different company. Ideally you will be able to qualify for a company's "select preferred" or "super preferred" rates. So if you disagree with the company's assessment of your health, don't be bashful about applying with a different company. It can't hurt.

The following are some of the major health concerns that will affect your ability to purchase a policy and its price:

- Smoking tobacco

- Hazardous occupation, such as high-rise construction or underground mining

- AIDS

- Alzheimer's disease

- Coronary artery disease

- Liver disease

Premium Cost

Price is an obvious consideration when selecting an insurance policy. You clearly don't want to pay any more than you have to for a policy. And based on your financial situation, some policies may even require premiums that are too high for you to afford. This is why it definitely pays to shop around. As you will see, you'll almost always find insurers charging different prices for exactly the same policy coverage. Sometimes this is based on differing perceptions of your health (as discussed previously). Sometimes it is based on the insurance company's claims experience. But usually it will have more to do with the perceived quality of the company.

An established insurer that has built a reputation for reasonable premiums, prompt payment of claims, and strong financial stability will be able to charge more than others without these perceived qualities. Conversely, a relatively new insurer may choose to offer lower premiums in order to break into the market. Or, an insurer whose sales are slipping may lower premiums in a bid to gain more market share. For the most part, these factors are beyond your control. As such, you should focus your efforts on finding the best price possible from a stable and reputable insurer.

Financial Stability of the Insurer

Purchasing a life insurance policy won't do your loved ones much good if the insurance company issuing it is out of business when they go to file their claim. State regulators require insurers to set aside reserves so that they can pay claims as they materialize. Nevertheless, some insurers don't set aside enough money, or they may lose money on their operations due to insufficient premiums or high expense levels. Any one of these factors can ultimately drive an insurer out of business.

For these reasons, Weiss Ratings recommends you purchase your insurance policy from a company receiving a Safety Rating of A+, A, A-, or B+ whenever possible. These recommended companies by definition offer excellent financial stability and have the resources necessary to deal with severe economic conditions. Make sure you are looking at the company's Safety Rating though. A "B+" rating from other rating agencies actually means the company is financially vulnerable to failure. (See "What Our Ratings Mean" for more information.)

Reputation of the Insurer

Many people feel it is worth it to pay a little extra in order to purchase an insurance policy from a company that they know or have heard of. Just be sure that you don't confuse the company's reputation with its advertising budget. A few notable insurers spend a lot of money on television ads proclaiming their superiority when in fact they would be better served putting that money toward improving their financial stability or speeding up their claims payment process.

The best indicator of a company's true (not perceived) reputation is past experience. So if you want information on a company's customer service or speed in paying claims, the best place to turn is past and present customers. Depending upon how much effort you want to invest, you can ask your friends and neighbors if they would recommend their insurer, you can conduct an Internet search for commentary from disgruntled customers, and you can even contact your state department of insurance and request a complaint history on a company you may be considering.

Previous Relationship with a Company or Agent

Of course you probably already have an established relationship with a particular company or insurance agent for your auto or homeowners insurance. Are you happy with them? If so, then you may want to purchase your life insurance policy from the same agent/company for the added convenience or peace of mind. Just make sure you know exactly how much more you are paying for that convenience. If it will save you hundreds of dollars per year, you may decide it's worth going somewhere else to buy your life insurance.

Agent's Sales Presentation

State law requires that the agent or company selling insurance must provide you with a "policy presentation" that clearly spells out what you are getting and how much it will cost you. While this is an opportunity for you to get a better feel for the company, don't be misled by fancy, colorful presentations. Instead focus on how promptly the sales rep returns your call and how well they are able to answer your questions. This may be your only chance to personally gauge their customer service and expertise.

Once you've identified one or more policies that appear to meet all of your needs, the next step is to contact an agent or sales representative to begin the paperwork process and confirm exactly which policy premium you qualify for. At this point, you essentially have three options:

- Contacting the insurer

- Contacting an agent

- Buying through the Internet

Regardless of which way you go, the application process won't cost you anything more than your time. So if you are considering policies from multiple companies, you will probably want to move forward on all of them at the same time so as not to drag the process out.

Contacting the Insurer

Call the insurer directly to access information about them or to inquire about obtaining an application to fill out to receive a written quote from the company. This is probably the most direct route since you are essentially avoiding the middleman. Be aware though that some insurers will not sell a policy directly to you. In such cases, they will most likely direct you to an insurance agent in your area who can help you.

If the insurer does sell direct to consumers, you will be transferred to a sales rep who will serve as your primary point of contact. Some company sales reps are commissioned and others are not, so be careful if the rep starts pushing you to increase your policy coverage amount or the length of your term. He could be looking out for your best interests, but more likely than not, he's trying to boost his commission.

Don't expect a lot of personal consultation if you pursue this route. The sales reps will take down your information and provide information about the policy back to you. However, it is very unlikely that he or she will be well versed enough to help you with a needs assessment or will take the time to consider what is best for you. You will essentially be dealing with an order taker, so if you're unsure of what you want, you might want to consider going through an agent instead.

Contacting an Agent

If you already have an agent, that's a great place to start assuming the companies he or she represents can offer competitive pricing. If you don't have an insurance agent or if he does not represent a specific policy of interest, then you'll need to find an agent who can help you.

You can start by calling the company's headquarters and asking them to refer you to an agent in your area. Or, you may try consulting a local telephone directory or conducting an Internet search based on the name of the specific insurance company. Unless the company is small or doesn't do much business in your state, this should give you a contact name.

Alternatively, you can always ask your own agent for a referral. Assuming he is cooperative, he can usually direct you to an insurance broker that represents the company you're looking at. And finally, if you haven't settled on a specific company or policy yet, then word-of-mouth is the best way to find a good insurance agent. Ask your relatives, friends, neighbors, and co-workers to recommend their insurance agent if he or she is any good.

When considering a specific agent, look for professional designations, such as Chartered Life Underwriter (CLU), Chartered Financial Consultant (ChFC) or Certified Financial Planner (CFP). Agents with these credentials are required to take yearly educational courses to keep them on top of insurance and financial planning issues. In addition, members of these professional organizations are also required to follow a code of conduct in order to keep their designations.

Once you find an agent, don't be shy about asking questions. He is going to make a nice commission when he sells you a policy, so don't feel bad about making him work a little to earn that commission. You may even be able to tap his brain for some broad financial planning advice during the process of selling you a policy.

Buying through the Internet

The advent and acceptance of doing business on the Internet has given do-it-yourselfers a new avenue for purchasing insurance. Many people find this route particularly appealing thanks to the comfortable setting, allowing you to proceed at your own pace and make your own decisions without a pushy salesman twisting your arm to boost his commission. Plus, you theoretically should be able to save money over the Internet since the company's sales commission is usually less than if you were purchasing through an agent.

The downside of buying through the Internet is the lack of one-on-one consultation that many people need in order to feel comfortable with their choices. There is a tremendous amount of information available to you at insurance-related websites like www.quickquote.com and www.insure.com. But pursuing this avenue means you have to do all of the work yourself. This might prove particularly arduous if you need help determining the amount of insurance you need or understanding your basic policy options.

If you're comfortable purchasing over the Internet, there are many websites that can provide you with term life quotes which you can then compare to determine which premium quoted and coverage granted is right for you. These include:

- www.insure.com
- www.insurance.com
- www.intelliquote.com

- www.lifeinsurancewiz.com
- www.quickquote.com
- www.termlifeamerica.com
- www.reliaquote.com

be able to save money over the Internet since the company's sales commission is usually less than if you were purchasing through an agent.

The downside of buying through the Internet is the lack of one-on-one consultation that many people need in order to feel comfortable with their choices. There is a tremendous amount of information available to you at insurance-related websites like www.quickquote.com and www.insure.com. But pursuing this avenue means you have to do all of the work yourself. This might prove particularly arduous if you need help determining the amount of insurance you need or understanding your basic policy options.

If you're comfortable purchasing over the Internet, there are many websites that can provide you with term life quotes which you can then compare to determine which premium quoted and coverage granted is right for you. These include:

- www.insure.com
- www.insurance.com
- www.insweb.com
- www.intelliquote.com
- www.termlifeamerica.com
- www.lifeinsurancewiz.com
- www.quickquote.com
- www.quotetermlife.com
- www.reliaquote.com

Part IV:

Weiss
Recommended List

Important Warnings and Cautions

1. A rating alone cannot tell the whole story. Please read the explanatory information contained in this publication. It is provided in order to give you an understanding of our rating philosophy, as well as paint a more complete picture of how we arrive at our opinion of a company's strengths and weaknesses.

2. Weiss Safety Ratings represent our opinion of a company's insolvency risk. As such, a high rating means we feel that the company has less chance of running into financial difficulties. A high rating is not a guarantee of solvency nor is a low rating a prediction of insolvency. Weiss Safety Ratings are not deemed to be a recommendation concerning the purchase or sale of the securities of any insurance company that is publicly owned.

3. Company performance is only one factor in determining a rating. Conditions in the marketplace and overall economic conditions are additional factors that may affect the company's financial strength. Therefore, a rating upgrade or downgrade does not necessarily reflect changes in the company's profits, capital or other financial measures, but may be due to external factors. Likewise, changes in Weiss Ratings' indexes may reflect changes in our risk assessment of business or economic conditions as well as changes in company performance.

4. All firms that have the same Weiss Safety Rating should be considered to be essentially equal in safety. This is true regardless of any differences in the underlying numbers which might appear to indicate greater strengths. Weiss Safety Rating already takes into account a number of lesser factors which, due to space limitations, cannot be included in this publication.

5. A good rating requires consistency. If a company is excellent on four indicators and fair on one, the company may receive a fair rating. This requirement is necessary due to the fact that fiscal problems can arise from any one of several causes including speculative investments, inadequate capital resources or operating losses.

6. We are an independent rating agency and do not depend on the cooperation of the companies we rate. Our data are derived, for the most part, from annual and quarterly financial statements that we obtain from federal banking regulators and state insurance commissioners. The latter may be supplemented by information insurance companies voluntarily provide upon request. Although we seek to maintain an open line of communication with the companies, we do not grant them the right to stop or influence publication of the ratings. This policy stems from the fact that this publication is designed for the protection of the consumer.

7. Affiliated companies do not automatically receive the same rating. We recognize that a troubled company may expect financial support from its parent or affiliates. Weiss Safety Ratings reflect our opinion of the measure of support that may become available to a subsidiary, if the subsidiary were to experience serious financial difficulties. In the case of a strong parent and a weaker subsidiary, the affiliate relationship will generally result in a higher rating for the subsidiary than it would have on a stand-alone basis. Seldom, however, would the rating be brought up to the level of the parent. This treatment is appropriate because we do not assume the parent would have either the resources or when there is a binding legal obligation for a parent corporation to honor the policy obligations of its subsidiaries, the possibility exists that the subsidiary could be sold and lose its parental support. Therefore, it is quite common for one affiliate to have a higher rating than another. This is another reason why it is especially important that you have the precise name of the company you are evaluating.

What Our Ratings Mean

A Excellent. The company offers excellent financial security. It has maintained a conservative stance in its investment strategies, business operations and underwriting commitments. While the financial position of any company is subject to change, we believe that this company has the resources necessary to deal with severe economic conditions.

B Good. The company offers good financial security and has the resources to deal with a variety of adverse economic conditions. It comfortably exceeds the minimum levels for all of our rating criteria, and is likely to remain healthy for the near future. However, in the event of a severe recession or major financial crisis, we feel that this assessment should be reviewed to make sure that the firm is still maintaining adequate financial strength.

C Fair. The company offers fair financial security and is currently stable. But during an economic downturn or other financial pressures, we feel it may encounter difficulties in maintaining its financial stability.

D Weak. The company currently demonstrates what, in our opinion, we consider to be significant weaknesses which could negatively impact policyholders. In an unfavorable economic environment, these weaknesses could be magnified.

E Very Weak. The company currently demonstrates what we consider to be significant weaknesses and has also failed some of the basic tests that we use to identify fiscal stability. Therefore, even in a favorable economic environment, it is our opinion that policyholders could incur significant risks.

F Failed. The company is deemed failed if it is either 1) under supervision of an insurance regulatory authority; 2) in the process of rehabilitation; 3) in the process of liquidation; or 4) voluntarily dissolved after disciplinary or other regulatory action by an insurance regulatory authority.

+ The plus sign is an indication that the company is in the upper third of the letter grade.

− The minus sign is an indication that the company is in the lower third of the letter grade

U Unrated Companies. The company is unrated for one or more of the following reasons: (1) total assets are less than $1 million; (2) premium income for the current year was less than $100,000; or (3) the company functions almost exclusively as a holding company rather than as an underwriter; or, (4) in our opinion, we do not have enough information to reliably issue a rating.

Weiss Recommended List

The following pages list Weiss Recommended Life Insurers. These life insurers currently receive a Safety Rating of A+, A, A-, or B+, indicating their strong financial position. Companies are listed by their Weiss Safety Rating and then alphabetically within each Safety Rating grouping.

If an insurer is not on this list, it should not be automatically assumed that the firm is weak. Indeed, there are many firms that have not achieved a B+ or better rating but are in relatively good condition with adequate resources to cover their risk. Not being included in this list should not be construed as a recommendation to cancel a policy.

To get Weiss Safety Rating for a company not included here, go to www.weissratings.com.

Name	The insurance company's legally registered name, which can sometimes differ from the name that the company uses for advertising. An insurer's name can be very similar to the name of other companies which may not be on this list, so make sure you note the exact name before contacting your agent.
Weiss Safety Rating	Our rating is measured on a scale from A to F and considers a wide range of factors. Highly rated companies are, in our opinion, less likely to experience financial difficulties than lower-rated firms. See "What Our Ratings Mean" for a definition of each rating category.
Domicile State	The state where the main office is located.
Website Address	The web address where you can contact the firm for additional information or for the location of local branches and/or registered agents.
Telephone	The telephone number to call for information on purchasing an insurance policy from the company.

Company	Domicile State	Website	Telephone
Safety Rating: A+			
American Family Life Ins Co	WI	www.amfam.com	(608) 249-2111
Chesapeake Life Ins Co	OK	www.healthmarketsinc.com	(817) 255-3100
Country Life Ins Co	IL	www.countryfinancial.com	(309) 821-3000
Physicians Mutual Ins Co	NE	www.physiciansmutual.com	(402) 633-1000
State Farm Life & Accident Asr Co	IL	www.statefarm.com	(309) 766-2311
State Farm Life Ins Co	IL	www.statefarm.com	(309) 766-2311
Teachers Ins & Annuity Asn of Am	NY	www.tiaa.org	(212) 490-9000
Safety Rating: A			
American Continental Ins Co	TN	www.aetnaseniorproducts.com	(800) 264-4000
American Family Life Asr Co of NY	NY	www.aflac.com	(706) 243-8708
Berkley Life & Health Ins Co	IA	www.berkley.com	(609) 584-6990
Direct General Life Ins Co	SC	www.directauto.com	(336) 435-2000
Empire Fidelity Investments L I C	NY	www.fidelity.com	(401) 292-4717
Federated Life Ins Co	MN	www.federatedinsurance.com	(507) 455-5200
Fidelity Investments Life Ins Co	UT	www.fidelity.com	(401) 292-4717
Frandisco Life Ins Co	GA	www.1ffc.com	(706) 886-7571
Garden State Life Ins Co	TX	www.americannational.com	(409) 763-4661
Guardian Life Ins Co of America	NY	www.guardianlife.com	(212) 919-8000
National Foundation Life Ins Co	TX	www.nfl-ins.com	(817) 878-3300
Sentry Life Ins Co	WI	www.sentry.com	(715) 346-6000
Shelterpoint Life Ins Co	NY	www.shelterpoint.com	(516) 829-8100
Southern Farm Bureau Life Ins Co	MS	www.sfbli.com	(601) 981-7422
Standard Life Ins Co of NY	NY	www.standard.com	(914) 989-4400
Safety Rating: A-			
Amica Life Ins Co	RI	www.amica.com	(800) 652-6422
Annuity Investors Life Ins Co	OH	www.massmutual.com	(513) 361-9000
Bluebonnet Life Ins Co	MS	No Website Available	(601) 664-4218
Central States H & L Co of Omaha	NE	www.cso.com	(402) 397-1111
Country Investors Life Asr Co	IL	www.countryfinancial.com	(309) 821-3000
Delaware American Life Ins Co	DE	www.metlife.com	(302) 594-2000
Farm Bureau Life Ins Co of Michigan	MI	www.farmbureauinsurance-mi.com	(517) 323-7000
Fidelity Security Life Ins Co	MO	www.fslins.com	(816) 756-1060
Fidelity Security Life Ins Co of NY	NY	www.fslins.com	(800) 821-7303
First Reliance Standard Life Ins Co	NY	www.reliancestandard.com	(212) 303-8400

Company	Domicile State	Website	Telephone

Safety Rating: A- (continued)

Company	Domicile State	Website	Telephone
National Benefit Life Ins Co	NY	www.nationalbenefitlife.com	(718) 361-3636
New York Life Ins Co	NY	www.newyorklife.com	(212) 576-7000
Pacific Life Ins Co	NE	www.pacificlife.com	(949) 219-3943
Parker Centennial Asr Co	WI	www.sentry.com	(715) 346-6000
Standard Security Life Ins Co of NY	NY	www.sslicny.com	(212) 355-4141
Swbc Life Ins Co	TX	www.swbc.com	(210) 321-7361
Trustmark Life Ins Co	IL	www.trustmarkcompanies.com	(847) 615-1500

Safety Rating: B+

Company	Domicile State	Website	Telephone
Advance Ins Co of Kansas	KS	www.advanceinsurance.com	(785) 273-9804
American Fidelity Asr Co	OK	americanfidelity.com	(405) 523-2000
American Health & Life Ins Co	TX	www.onemainsolutions.com	(800) 307-0048
Assurity Life Ins Co	NE	www.assurity.com	(402) 476-6500
Best Life & Health Ins Co	TX	www.bestlife.com	(949) 253-4080
Boston Mutual Life Ins Co	MA	www.bostonmutual.com	(781) 828-7000
Christian Fidelity Life Ins Co	TX	www.oxfordlife.com	(602) 263-6666
Cm Life Ins Co	CT	www.massmutual.com	(413) 788-8411
Companion Life Ins Co	SC	www.companionlife.com	(803) 735-1251
Companion Life Ins Co of CA	CA	www.thedoctors.com	(803) 735-1251
Enterprise Life Ins Co	TX	No Website Available	(817) 878-3300
Farm Bureau Life Ins Co	IA	www.fbfs.com	(515) 225-5400
Freedom Life Ins Co of America	TX	www.ushealthgroup.com	(817) 878-3300
Gerber Life Ins Co	NY	www.gerberlife.com	(914) 272-4000
Hm Life Ins Co	PA	www.hmig.com	(800) 328-5433
Hm Life Ins Co of New York	NY	www.hmig.com	(800) 328-5433
Illinois Mutual Life Ins Co	IL	www.illinoismutual.com	(309) 674-8255
Life Ins Co of Boston & New York	NY	www.lifeofboston.com	(800) 645-2317
M Life Ins Co	CO	www.mfin.com	(503) 414-7336
National Farmers Union Life Ins Co	TX	www.americo.com	(816) 391-2000
National Health Ins Co	TX	www.ngah-ngic.com	(888) 781-0580
Niagara Life & Health Ins Co	NY	No Website Available	(803) 735-1251
Northwestern Long Term Care Ins Co	WI	www.northwesternmutual.com	(414) 271-1444
Northwestern Mutual Life Ins Co	WI	www.northwesternmutual.com	(414) 271-1444
NY Life Ins & Annuity Corp	DE	No Website Available	(212) 576-7000
Nylife Ins Co of Arizona	AZ	www.newyorklife.com	(212) 576-7000
Old Republic Life Ins Co	IL	www.oldrepublic.com	(312) 346-8100

Company	Domicile State	Website	Telephone
Safety Rating: B+ (continued)			
Oxford Life Ins Co	AZ	www.oxfordlife.com	(602) 263-6666
Pacific Life & Annuity Co	AZ	www.pacificlife.com	(949) 219-3011
Pan American Asr Co	LA	www.palig.com	(504) 566-1300
Physicians Life Ins Co	NE	www.physiciansmutual.com	(402) 633-1000
Popular Life Re	PR	No Website Available	(787) 706-4111
Principal Life Ins Co	IA	www.principal.com	(515) 247-5111
Standard Ins Co	OR	www.standard.com	(971) 321-7000
Symetra National Life Ins Co	IA	www.symetra.com	(425) 256-8000
Tennessee Farmers Life Ins Co	TN	www.fbitn.com	(931) 388-7872
Trans Oceanic Life Ins Co	PR	tolic.com	(787) 620-2680
Trans World Asr Co	CA	www.twalife.com	(650) 348-2300
United Farm Family Life Ins Co	IN	www.infarmbureau.com	(317) 692-7200
United Home Life Ins Co	IN	www.unitedhomelife.com	(800) 428-3001
United National Life Ins Co of Am	IL	unlinsurance.com	(847) 803-5252
United World Life Ins Co	NE	www.mutualofomaha.com	(402) 342-7600
USAA Life Ins Co	TX	www.usaa.com	(210) 531-8722

Appendix

Life Insurance Needs Worksheet

Determining the amount of insurance you need is not an exact science. Nevertheless, the worksheet that follows will help you get to a good ballpark figure. If you've got a sizable estate though, or if you are uncomfortable following this worksheet, you should seek the advice of a qualified fee-only estate planner (see www.NAPFA.org for a list of estate planners near you).

Whatever you do, be sure to ignore any "rules of thumb" as a basis for your life insurance needs. A rule of thumb may be a shortcut to an answer, but you could wind up with an answer that will cost you unnecessarily, or conversely, leave your loved ones without adequate financial resources. Rules of thumb only apply to averages, and your particular circumstances may not be average.

Besides, determining how much life insurance you need is not that difficult. In concept, you're simply finding the difference between the amount of financial needs your family will require in the event of your passing and the amount of financial resources that would be available to them. See the "Life Insurance Needs" Worksheet to help you work through the process.

Just take it one step at a time. When addressing each line, consult the instructions starting on the next page and follow the worksheet for a clearer understanding of what that line should include. And if you get to a line that you don't know or can't readily determine, don't worry, ballpark figures will do. If it will make you more comfortable, you may even want to complete the worksheet under three scenarios: high, low, and middle. That should give you a range of benefit needs to work with.

In the end, you will probably choose to round up or round down to a "round number" anyway, so don't sweat the details.

Instructions for Life Insurance Needs Worksheet

Final Expenses

Line 1. **Funeral expenses**. A basic funeral without any extras should cost approximately $5,000. If you want your loved ones to splurge with lots of flowers, limousines, and the works, that could easily ratchet the cost up to around $10,000. Of course, you can go well over $10,000 if you want an extravagant funeral. For estimating purposes though, between $5,000 and $10,000 should be sufficient.

Line 2. **Probate expenses**. These are the expenses required to settle your estate. If you have a relatively simple will or few assets, then this cost will be less. Also, any assets held in trust accounts, qualified pension plans, or life insurance policies generally bypass the probate process, lessening the expense. If you have a large amount of investments and other assets that are subject to probate, then the cost will be higher, so you may want to consult your family attorney to get a more accurate estimate of these costs.

Line 3. **Estate taxes**. Most families need not worry about estate taxes. If you have a large estate, your family lawyer or financial consultant has probably already advised you on the amount of taxes you are likely to pay. If not, we recommend you consult with a fee-only estate planner who will help estimate your estate taxes and determine the appropriate amount of life insurance for your needs.

Line 4. **Uninsured Medical Costs**. Depending on your health insurance plan and the ultimate cause of your demise, you could very easily rack up some sizable medical expenses, particularly if you contract a terminal illness. These costs are almost impossible to predict, but if you've got a good health insurance plan, you can probably assume $0 or some nominal amount. At the other extreme, if your health insurance does not cover terminal illness, then you may want to estimate $50,000 to $100,000.

Line 5. **Total Final Expenses**. Total lines 1 through 4.

Existing Debts

Line 6. <u>Credit cards</u>. Include any balances that you normally carry, or expect to carry, on your credit cards from month to month.

Line 7. <u>Auto Loans</u>. Include the outstanding balance on any auto loans, including both your car and your spouse's car.

Line 8. <u>Mortgage</u>. Include the entire outstanding balance of your family mortgage, regardless of whether your dependents might decide to pay it off with the proceeds from your life insurance policy. Also, if you plan to trade up to a larger house with a larger mortgage, use the estimated amount of the new mortgage instead.

Line 9. <u>Other Loans</u>. Include the outstanding balances from any other loans, including home equity loans, boat loans, student loans, etc.

Line 10. <u>Property taxes</u>. For the purposes of this worksheet, use the approximate annual amount of property tax you expect to pay in the current year.

Line 11. <u>Total Existing Debts</u>. Total lines 6 through 10.

Future Expenses

Line 12. <u>Income needs</u>. These are your family's basic recurring expenses for food, clothing, utilities, gas and auto repairs, medical care, etc. less any income that will still be available to the family from other sources. Do not include your mortgage payments, but do include your property taxes and homeowner's insurance. This is probably the most difficult amount to estimate, so you may want to arrive at a range from high to low.

- First, add up the approximate amount of all monthly expenses your family would need to continue paying. You can get a good handle on this by looking at the checks you've paid over the last few months and averaging them to arrive at a monthly average.

- Next, determine what monthly income you expect your family to continue to receive after your death. This can include Social Security survivor benefits, pension plan benefits, your spouse's monthly income, etc. Don't include investment income or income from retirement accounts though. Those will be factored in later.

- Then, subtract the monthly income amount from your family's monthly expenses to determine a net monthly income need, and multiply this difference by twelve to get the annual amount of income needed.

- Finally, multiply this annual amount by the number of years you reasonably expect your dependents to need the income. If your children are grown and your spouse is in his or her 50s, then you might assume 20 to 30 years. On the other hand, if your primary reason for buying insurance is to provide for your young children, then use the number of years until your youngest child turns 18 or would graduate from college.

Line 13.   Emergency fund. Many financial planners suggest having an emergency fund of at least two to six months of after-tax income. Determine your current after-tax monthly income and multiply that number by two at the low end or six at the high end.

Line 14.   Child-care expenses. Do you have young children in day care or children in a private school? If so, estimate the annual cost for each child and multiply that by the number of years remaining before the child leaves day care or private school. Total this expected expense for all children.

Line 15.   College tuition. How much do you expect to contribute toward your children's college education? Be sure to consider room and board, books, transportation, and personal expenses in addition to the actual tuition costs. Tuition varies widely depending upon the college, but you can get national averages for public and private college tuition costs at www.collegeboard.com.

Line 16.   Total Future Expenses. Total lines 12 through 15.

Line 17.   Total Financial Requirements. Total lines 5, 11, and 16. This is the estimated total amount of money your dependents will need before considering any existing family assets.

Financial Resources

Line 18.   Cash and savings. Include the current balances of any family checking and savings accounts, including CDs, but excluding retirement accounts.

Line 19.   Real estate equity. If you own any investment properties or a second home, this is the difference between the estimated market value of those properties and the amount you still owe on any loans used to purchase them. Do not include the equity in your primary residence since those funds will not be available to your dependents unless they first sell the house.

Line 20. <u>Securities</u>. Include the current market value for all stocks, bonds, mutual funds, savings bonds, or other marketable securities that you own, excluding any investments owned in retirement accounts.

Line 21. <u>Retirement accounts</u>. Include the current balances in your IRA accounts, Keogh plans, 401(k) plans, lump-sum pensions, and other retirement accounts.

Line 22. <u>Current life insurance</u>. Include the benefit amount of any existing life insurance policies payable upon your death. Be sure to include policies provided by your employer.

Line 23. <u>Other assets</u>. Do you have any other assets that your family could sell off to raise money in a pinch? If so, include any assets not already included above.

Line 24. <u>Total Financial Resources</u>. Total lines 18 through 23.

Line 25. <u>Total Financial Requirements</u>. Copy over the amount from line 17.

Line 26. <u>Total Financial Resources</u>. Copy over the amount from line 24.

Line 27. <u>Insurance Needed</u>. Subtract line 26 from line 25. This is the estimated amount of insurance needed in order for your dependents to maintain their existing standard of living

From here, you may want to recompute the insurance needs based on a different standard of living or using other assumptions. This will give you a range of need to work from in finding a number that you are comfortable with and can afford.

One caveat about the worksheet: For simplicity sake, this worksheet does not take into consideration inflation or the time value of money. This may not be a concern if the family's income from wages and investments keeps pace with inflation. In a hyper inflationary environment though, you would want to increase the amount of insurance needed to compensate for inflation's impact on future expenses.

Life Insurance Needs Worksheet

Financial Requirements	Example	You
Final Expenses		
1. Funeral expenses	10,000	
2. Probate Expenses	3,000	
3. Estate taxes	0	
4. Uninsured medical costs	0	
5. Total	**13,000**	
Existing Debts		
6. Credit cards	8,000	
7. Auto Loans	16,000	
8. Mortgages	100,000	
9. Other loans	20,000	
10. Property taxes	2,000	
11. Total	**146,000**	
Future Expenses		
12. Income needs	120,000	
13. Emergency fund	25,000	
14. Child-care expenses	30,000	
15. College tuition	60,000	
16. Total	**235,000**	
17. **Total Financial Requirements** (Line 5 + Line 11 + Line 16)	**394,000**	
18. Cash and savings	9,000	
19. Real estate equity	36,000	
20. Securities	6,000	
21. Retirement accounts	105,000	
22. Current life insurance	50,000	
23. Other assets	12,000	
24. **Total Financial Resources**	**218,000**	
25. Total Financial Requirements (Line 17)	394,000	
26. Total Financial Resources (Line 24)	218,000	
27. **Insurance Needed** (Line 25 – Line 26)	**176,000**	

State Insurance Commissioners' Departmental Contact Information

State	Official's Title	Website Address	Phone Number
Alabama	Commissioner	www.aldoi.gov	(334) 269-3550
Alaska	Director	https://www.commerce.alaska.gov/web/ins/	(907) 269-7900
Arizona	Director	https://insurance.az.gov/	(602) 364-3100
Arkansas	Commissioner	www.insurance.arkansas.gov	(501) 371-2600
California	Commissioner	www.insurance.ca.gov	(916) 492-3500
Colorado	Commissioner	https://dora.colorado.gov/	(303) 894-7499
Connecticut	Commissioner	https://portal.ct.gov/cid	(860) 297-3800
Delaware	Commissioner	https://insurance.delaware.gov/	(302) 674-7300
Dist. of Columbia	Commissioner	http://disb.dc.gov/	(202) 727-8000
Florida	Commissioner	www.floir.com/	(850) 413-3140
Georgia	Commissioner	www.oci.ga.gov/	(404) 656-2070
Hawaii	Commissioner	http://cca.hawaii.gov/ins/	(808) 586-2790
Idaho	Director	www.doi.idaho.gov	(208) 334-4250
Illinois	Director	/www2.illinois.gov/	(217) 558-2757
Indiana	Commissioner	www.in.gov/idoi/	(317) 232-2385
Iowa	Commissioner	https://iid.iowa.gov/	(515) 654-6600
Kansas	Commissioner	https://insurance.kansas.gov/	(785) 296-3071
Kentucky	Commissioner	https://insurance.ky.gov/ppc/new_default.aspx	(502) 564-3630
Louisiana	Commissioner	www.ldi.la.gov/	(225) 342-5900
Maine	Superintendent	www.maine.gov/pfr/insurance/	(207) 624-8475
Maryland	Commissioner	http://insurance.maryland.gov/Pages/default.aspx	(410) 468-2000
Massachusetts	Commissioner	https://www.mass.gov/orgs/division-of-insurance	(617) 521-7794
Michigan	Director	http://www.michigan.gov/difs	(517) 284-8800
Minnesota	Commissioner	http://mn.gov/commerce/	(651) 539-1500
Mississippi	Commissioner	http://www.mid.ms.gov/	(601) 359-3569
Missouri	Director	www.insurance.mo.gov	(573) 751-4126
Montana	Commissioner	http://csimt.gov/	(406) 444-2040
Nebraska	Director	www.doi.nebraska.gov/	(402) 471-2201
Nevada	Commissioner	www.doi.nebraska.gov/	(775) 687-0700
New Hampshire	Commissioner	www.nh.gov/insurance/	(603) 271-2261
New Jersey	Commissioner	www.state.nj.us/dobi/	(609) 292-7272
New Mexico	Superintendent	www.osi.state.nm.us/	(505) 827-4601
New York	Superintendent	www.dfs.ny.gov/	(212) 709-3500
North Carolina	Commissioner	https://www.ncdoi.gov/	(919) 807-6000
North Dakota	Commissioner	https://www.insurance.nd.gov/	(701) 328-2440
Ohio	Director	www.insurance.ohio.gov	(614) 644-2658
Oklahoma	Commissioner	https://www.oid.ok.gov/	(405) 521-2828
Oregon	Insurance Commissioner	http://dfr.oregon.gov/Pages/index.aspx	(503) 947-7980
Pennsylvania	Commissioner	www.insurance.pa.gov/	(717) 787-7000
Puerto Rico	Commissioner	https://ocs.pr.gov/English/Pages/default.aspx	(787) 304-8686
Rhode Island	Superintendent	https://dbr.ri.gov/contact/	(401) 462-9500
South Carolina	Director	www.doi.sc.gov	(803) 737-6160
South Dakota	Director	http://dlr.sd.gov/insurance/default.aspx	(605) 773-3563
Tennessee	Commissioner	http://tn.gov/commerce/	(615) 741-2241
Texas	Commissioner	www.tdi.texas.gov/	(512) 676-6000
Utah	Commissioner	www.insurance.utah.gov	(801) 957-9200
Vermont	Commissioner	www.dfr.vermont.gov/	(802) 828-3301
Virgin Islands	Lieutenant Governor	https://ltg.gov.vi/	(340) 774-7166
Virginia	Commissioner	https://scc.virginia.gov/pages/Home	(804) 371-9741
Washington	Commissioner	www.insurance.wa.gov	(360) 725-7000
West Virginia	Commissioner	www.wvinsurance.gov	(304) 558-3354
Wisconsin	Commissioner	https://oci.wi.gov/Pages/Homepage.aspx	(608) 266-3586
Wyoming	Commissioner	http://doi.wyo.gov/	(307) 777-7401

Glossary

Beneficiary – The person or party to whom the cash payout is made upon the death of the insured.

Chartered Financial Consultant (ChFC) – A professional designation awarded to professional financial consultants. In addition to advising clients on life insurance matters, ChFCs are also versed in general financial planning. In order to maintain this designation, the professional must participate in continuing education each year.

Chartered Financial Planner (CFP) – A professional designation awarded to professional financial planners. In addition to advising clients on life insurance matters, CFPs are also versed in general financial planning. In order to maintain this designation, the professional must participate in continuing education each year.

Chartered Life Underwriter (CLU) – A professional designation awarded to insurance professionals specializing in life insurance. In order to maintain this designation, the professional must participate in continuing education each year.

Convertible Policy – A policy that gives the policy owner the option to switch the policy to a permanent insurance policy.

Death Benefit – The stated amount of money an insurance company agrees to pay under an insurance policy upon the death of an insured.

Duration – The maximum period of time over which the coverage continues if the insured survives and the policy remains in effect.

Estate Taxes – Taxes assessed upon the value of an estate at the time it is passed to the deceased's heirs (other than a spouse).

Evidence of Insurability – Proof that an insured person continues to be an insurable risk. An applicant is usually required to undergo medical exams or otherwise provide a health history.

Face Amount – A financial consultant who provides his services for an hourly fee rather than receiving a commission on assets invested.

Insured – The person whose life is covered under an insurance policy.

Mortality Rates – Death rates that can be reasonably anticipated for a group of people at certain ages. These rates indicate how many people in each age group are expected to die in a specific year. The rates are normally expressed as the number of deaths per 1,000 people.

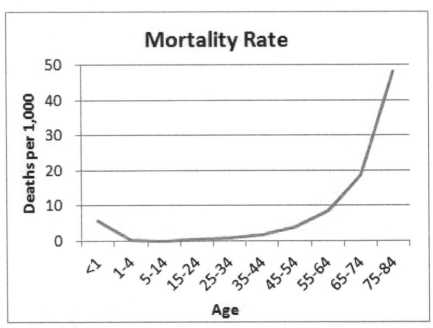

Source: National Vital Statistics Reports, Vol. 64, No. 2, January 16, 2016

The graph to the right shows that mortality rates are somewhat high for infants through age one (about 6 per 1,000), decline and level off through age 35 (about 2 per 1,000), increase slowly to age 55 (about 9 per 1,000) and then increase drastically after that (about 48 per 1,000 at age 75). Thus, as age increases, so does the chance of death. As a result, it is more expensive to insure the risk of death as a person gets older.

Permanent Life Insurance – A life insurance policy that remains in force for the insured's lifetime.

Policy Term – The number of years a life insurance policy remains in force under the original contractual agreement.

Policyholder/Policyowner – The person or party that owns an insurance policy. In most cases, the insured is also the policyholder. In some cases, however, the policyholder is not the insured. For example, a parent may buy an insurance policy on his or her child. This is known as a third-party policy.

Premium – A specified amount of money an insurer charges in exchange for its promise to pay a policy benefit when the insured dies. Premiums can be paid annually, semi-annually, quarterly, or monthly.

Premium Payer – The person or party who purchases the policy.

Renewable Policy – A policy that gives the policy owner the option to continue the coverage for an additional term.

Rider – An addendum to a policy that can either expand or limit the policy's benefits with a corresponding increase or decrease in premium.

Term Life Insurance – A life insurance policy that remains in force for a limited period of time. Term policies may generally be renewed, albeit at a higher premium rate.

Renewable Policy – A policy that gives the policy owner the option to continue the coverage for an additional term.

Rider – An addendum to a policy that can either expand or limit the policy's benefits with a corresponding increase or decrease in premium.

Term Life Insurance – A life insurance policy that remains in force for a limited period of time. Term policies may generally be renewed, albeit at a higher premium rate.

Weiss Safety Rating – An assessment of the insurance company's overall financial stability, indicating its financial capacity to pay future claims. See What Our Ratings Mean.